T0131230

Lincoln at Two Hundred

Why We Still Read the Sixteenth President

Walter Berns

AEI Bradley Lecture
February 9, 2009

With an introduction by Leon R. Kass

The AEI Press

Publisher for the American Enterprise Institute

WASHINGTON, D.C.

Distributed to the Trade by National Book Network, 15200 NBN Way, Blue Ridge Summit, PA 17214. To order call toll free 1-800-462-6420 or 1-717-794-3800. For all other inquiries please contact the AEI Press, 1150 Seventeenth Street, N.W., Washington, D.C. 20036 or call 1-800-862-5801.

Library of Congress Cataloging-in-Publication Data

Berns, Walter, 1919-
  Lincoln at two hundred : why we still read the sixteenth president / Walter Berns.
      p. cm.
   ISBN-13: 978-0-8447-4364-6 (pbk.)
   ISBN-10: 0-8447-4364-X (pbk.)
   ISBN-13: 978-0-8447-4365-3 (ebook)
   ISBN-10: 0-8447-4365-8 (ebook)
  1. Lincoln, Abraham, 1809–1865—Influence. 2. Lincoln, Abraham, 1809–1865—Political and social views. 3. Presidents—United States—Biography. 4. Political leadership—United States. I. Title.
   E457.2.B47 2010
   973.7092--dc22
   [B]

                                                        2010027296

14 13 12 11 10   1 2 3 4 5

Contents

Introduction

Leon R. Kass

In the Chicago of my boyhood, the birthday of Abraham Lincoln was a public school holiday, celebrated not on some wandering and anonymous "Presidents' Day," but always and memorably on February 12, the date of Lincoln's birth. Portraits of Lincoln—and also of George Washington—adorned our classrooms. Even before we knew the reason, we learned to admire, even to revere, this unlikely-looking hero: Honest Abe, the Great Emancipator, the man who saved the Union and freed the slaves. In assigned biographies, written for children, we learned about Lincoln's improbable rise from humblest origins, his love of learning and remarkable wit, and his gift with words, some of which we had to memorize. We learned of his determined leadership in waging and winning the Civil War, for which success he paid the ultimate price. And we grieved over his death, with the help of Walt Whitman's "O Captain, My Captain." For us, Abraham Lincoln was the "hero of heroes," the memory of whose life and words inspired us to love what was best about our country and to envision the noblest possibilities of our humanity for ourselves.

Now, more than seven score years and two dozen presidents later, our grandchildren are reared on different fare. Today, the heroes of old are under suspicion, brought down to size by several generations of revisionist scholars, who delight in "demythologizing" the American past and who have little use for the "great man" theories of history. The only American whose birthday we annually celebrate by name is Martin Luther King Jr., martyred for his courageous and eloquent opposition to racial segregation. Yet Dr. King was quick to recognize Lincoln's greatness and, moreover, his own debt to him. It is not by chance that his greatest speech ("I Have a Dream," August 28, 1963) was delivered in the nation's capital on the steps of the Lincoln Memorial, with Daniel Chester French's majestic rendering of the Great Emancipator seated literally and figuratively—and, we imagine, approvingly—right behind him.

Loyalty to the truth and our own self-respect require that we, too, get the story straight. Happily, the recent bicentennial of Lincoln's birth provided a perfect opportunity to remind ourselves of what we Americans owe to this extraordinary man. And Walter Berns seized the occasion and made the most of it. In this essay, first given as a lecture at the American Enterprise Institute on February 9, 2009, in his ninetieth year (I was privileged to hear it delivered), Professor Berns shows us, vividly and movingly, why Abraham Lincoln remains—and should remain—the hero of the American people.

Both by his life and by his thought, Walter Berns has been prepared to be our teacher on the subject of America and its heroes. He remembers a Memorial Day parade down Chicago's Michigan Avenue in 1926 and the impressive sight of aged Union veterans feebly carrying the regimental standards. He enlisted in the Navy before Pearl Harbor and served at sea during the entire course of World War II. The American Founding and constitutional law have been the center of his life's work as scholar and teacher. And Abraham Lincoln has been his man, the subject of many courses taught and articles written. For Lincoln has long been for Walter Berns the touchstone for thinking not only about American politics and patriotism, but also about human greatness.

In this moving tribute, the fruit of life-long study and reflection, Professor Berns offers us additional reasons for sharing his regard for Lincoln, a man supreme in both word and deed. Homer, it has been well said, was the poet or maker of the Greeks. Through his tales of gods and heroes, he not only showed them exemplars of stunning manliness, he also taught them what to think about their place and posture in the whole and the meaning of their humanity. As we learn from Walter Berns, Abraham Lincoln may be said to be the poet or maker of the Americans, both by teaching us what to think about our place and posture in the world and the meaning of our humanity, but also by his own heroic example of what it takes to defend, preserve, and live up to the highest principles of our common life.

Lincoln at Two Hundred
Why We Still Read the Sixteenth President

Walter Berns

More has been written about Abraham Lincoln than about any other president or, for that matter, any other American. The amount is prodigious: no fewer than 16,000 books and goodness knows how many journal articles. I cannot claim to have read more than a portion of this vast literature, and I very much doubt that I can say anything about Lincoln that has not already been said by someone, somewhere, sometime. Yet I am obliged to say something.

What accounts for the extraordinary interest in him? Well, he was an extraordinary man; he did things ordinary men don't do. For example, Lincoln's law partner reports how, while the other lawyers on circuit and the circuit judge were asleep, Lincoln would lie on the floor, with a lamp, studying Euclid's *Elements*, the geometry book which begins with definitions—e.g., "a point is that which has no part," followed by postulates and axioms, and then (and finally) by propositions, two sorts of propositions: problems and theorems. These propositions have then to be demonstrated, which is done diagrammatically, showing, in the one case, that the problem is solved, and, in the second, that the theorem is true.

All very interesting, and for some purposes, very important—the *Elements* is part of the Great Books curriculum; indeed, for almost two thousand years (until Descartes), Euclid *was* geometry—but what has it to do with the practice of law in Illinois in the 1840s? My point is, only an unusual intellectual curiosity could have led a backwoods lawyer to pick up Euclid's *Elements* and proceed to master it. Lincoln was different, and he had to know it.

Imagine, if you will, what it was like for this man to live in a place like New Salem, Illinois, in the 1830s, a town without books, without civilization, without anyone like himself with whom he might talk. Springfield, where he moved in 1837, was not much better. Yet, in both places, something drove him to get his hands on books, not only Euclid's geometry, but history, grammar, Shakespeare, and poetry.

Lincoln was an avid reader of poetry, beginning with the poems of Scotland's Robert Burns and continuing with those of England's George Gordon, Lord Byron. He started this reading in New Salem and Springfield and continued it in the White House, where he could get books from the Library of Congress. But what has "My Heart's in the Highlands" to do with the relief or provisioning of Fort Sumter? And what has Byron's "Don Juan" to do with emancipating slaves? Perhaps the best known passage in "Don Juan" is this: "A little still she strove, and much repented, and whispering 'I will ne'er consent'—consented." What has this to do with any of the problems that crossed Lincoln's White House desk? Nothing at all, of course. I mention it only because it tells us something about the sort of man he was. He also read the Bible, and seems to have known it well.

Burns, Byron, Bible: no one going to school with them is likely to have a tin ear. This was surely true of Lincoln. Their influence on him was evident, not in what he said, but in how he said it—in the rhythm or music of his speech. I'll have more to say about this in due course.

—⁓—

Lincoln was, of course, president in an extraordinary time, but so were Woodrow Wilson and Franklin D. Roosevelt. He was assassinated while in office, but so were James Garfield, William McKinley, and John F. Kennedy. Admittedly, there was something unusual or special about Lincoln's assassination. There was something profoundly political about it, and Lincoln may have foreseen it; he surely had forebodings of it. For example, he had the habit of quoting these words from Shakespeare's *King Richard the Second*: "For God's sake, let us sit upon the ground And tell sad stories of the death of kings . . . . all murder'd." What should one make of this?

Senator Charles Sumner reported—and so did the French diplomat the Marquis de Chambrun—that, upon returning from Richmond and a visit with General Grant the day before General Robert E. Lee's surrender at Appomattox, and knowing that the war was effectively over, Lincoln twice recited the following lines from Shakespeare's *Macbeth*:

> Duncan is in his grave;
> After life's fitful fever, he sleeps well;
> Treason has done his worst; nor steel, nor poison,
> Malice domestic, foreign levy, nothing
> Can touch him further.

Apparently, Lincoln saw himself as Duncan. Sumner thought so. If not, why did he quote this passage, not once, but twice, and at this time? (*Macbeth* was Lincoln's favorite play. As he said to a well-known Shakespearean actor, "Nothing equals *Macbeth*, it is wonderful.")

Of course, Lincoln did great things, greater than anything done by Wilson or Roosevelt, or by Garfield, McKinley, or Kennedy; he freed the slaves and saved the Union, and because he saved the Union, he was able to free the slaves.

Beyond this, however, it seems to me that our extraordinary interest in him, and esteem for him, has to do with what he said, and how he said it. And much of this had to do with the Union: what it was and why it was worth the saving.

———

Lincoln saved the Union by fighting and winning the war, of course; but his initial step was the decision to go to war in the first place. This was not a popular decision, and certainly not an easy one. His predecessor, the incompetent fool James Buchanan, believed that the states had no right to secede from the Union, but that there was nothing he could do about it if they did. Or, as Senator William H. Seward put it—he was commenting on Buchanan's last Message to Congress on December 3, 1860—"the states had no right to secede, unless they wanted to, and the president had the duty to enforce the law, unless someone opposed him." Thus, by the time Lincoln took office, seven southern states had seceded, and nothing had been done about it—nothing about their seizure of federal forts, arsenals, and naval facilities. Six of those states had formed a new government, with a constitution, a congress and president; they were, as we say, "in business." Led by South Carolina, they claimed to be doing only what they and the other colonies had done in 1776, and, on the whole, Buchanan agreed with them. Besides, to oppose them would probably bring on the war, and Buchanan had no stomach for that. As president, he had sworn an oath to "preserve, protect, and defend the Constitution of the United States," and to this end, he was given the powers of commander-in-chief. Yet he was the last man to use them.

It was otherwise with Lincoln. He knew very well that the time had come when the only way to save the Union was to go to war. But he hesitated to say so publicly. Could he say it and retain the support of the people who had voted for him? For the abolitionists, slavery was a sin, and the slaveholders sinners. But their leading spokesman, William Lloyd Garrison, was no friend of the Union. He said the Constitution was "a covenant with death and an agreement with hell," and once set fire to a copy of it, uttering the evangelist battle cry: "And let the people say, amen." Garrison and his friends were of no help to Lincoln. During the Fort Sumter crisis, Garrison said that "all Union saving efforts are simply idiotic."

Nor could Lincoln expect any help from his home-state newspaper, the *Chicago Tribune*. If South Carolina wanted to secede, the Tribune said in an editorial, "let her go." The country's leading anti-slavery editor, Horace Greeley of the *New York Tribune*, said much the same thing. As he put it, "if the Cotton States shall become satisfied they can do better out of the Union than in it, we insist on letting them go." But suppose we had let the southern states go.

With them would have gone almost all the slaves, gone to what claimed to be another country, a foreign country. How, then, could the abolitionists free them, except by going to war with that new country? The self-righteous Greeley did not say—perhaps he intended to enter into "real" negotiations with the Confederates— but it was his desire to *avoid* war that led him to say what he said.

Another problem facing Lincoln was this: The people of the North, especially the Republicans, were almost all anti-slavery, but they were also, almost all of them, anti-Negro. This prejudice was reflected in the laws adopted by the northern states, among them Illinois, Indiana, and Iowa, laws forbidding Negroes—*free* Negroes—from entering or remaining in the state. These Yankees, as they were soon to be known, obviously did not want Negroes in their neighborhoods, something their politicians could not afford to ignore.

Then—I'm speaking here of the situation Lincoln faced before taking office—there was the question of those slave states that had *not*, or not *yet*, seceded, specifically the border states of Virginia, Maryland, Missouri, Kentucky. What would these states do if he used force against the others? Later on, Lincoln was to say that he hoped God was on the side of the Union, but that he *had* to have Kentucky. Without it, there would be no chance of winning the civil war. (Look at a map.)

And, finally, there was the effort, a desperate, last-chance effort, to avoid the war by way of compromise. This is significant, and deserves to be treated in detail. On January 16, 1861, a mere six weeks before Lincoln's inauguration, the Kentuckian John Crittenden, on behalf of a Senate committee that included Democrats Stephen A. Douglas of Illinois and Jefferson Davis of Mississippi, as well as Republicans Benjamin Wade of Ohio and William Seward of New York, proposed a set of six constitutional amendments that—I mention only the major provisions—(1) guaranteed slavery in the states where it existed against future interference by the federal government, (2) denied Congress any power to interfere with the interstate slave trade, and (3)—and here is what proved to be the sticking point—prohibited slavery in the territories north of the

Missouri Compromise line, but protected slavery south of the line "*in all territories now held, or hereafter acquired.*"

Obviously, this was not much of a compromise; by giving them so much, the southern Democrats could be expected eagerly to support the amendments. For some reason, however—probably to avoid the war—the proposal also had the support of some important Republicans, including businessmen and Wall Street bankers. But Lincoln said *no.* "Let there be no compromise on the question of extending slavery," he wrote to his Republican friends in Congress. "The instant you do, they have us under again; all our labor is lost. . . . Douglas is sure to be again trying to bring in his 'Pop. Sov.' Have none of it. The tug has to come & better now than later." That tug came, and with it came the war.

———*∿∿*———

Question: Would Lincoln have taken so hard a line, or refused all compromise, had he anticipated that the war would take the lives of—the number is appalling—some 620,000 Americans? Probably not. (Nor, I suspect, would the southern states have seceded had they anticipated the price they would pay.) Intransigent, Lincoln surely was, but before blaming him for this, consider the alternative to war. What was at stake?

Lincoln stated the essential point time and again (and best, because succinctly, in his speech at the Cooper Institute in New York in February 1860): We Republicans, he said, think slavery wrong, and ought to be restricted, and they, the Southerners, think it right, and ought to be extended. "Their thinking it right," he said, "and our thinking it wrong, is the precise fact upon which depends the whole controversy."

And, by this time, a month or so before Lincoln took office, it was possible to know and state with sufficient precision what the extension of slavery would involve. First, according to the Crittenden proposal, slavery was to be protected south of the Missouri line "in all territories now held, *or hereafter acquired,*" and by this they meant territories not then, or not yet, part of the

United States. What were these territories? Well, Cuba, for instance—the Democrats had long had their eyes on it; in 1854, they tried to buy it (the Ostend proposal); and in 1860, their party platforms, the Northern or Douglas Democrats and the Southern or Breckinridge Democrats, called for its acquisition. And not only Cuba, but Mexico, or the part if it we had not already "acquired," and other places in Central America. But that's not all they had in mind.

There was a time when the Southerners were satisfied with the protection of slavery in some—the southern part—of the Louisiana Purchase territory; this was in 1820, when the Missouri compromise was adopted. And later, after the passage of the Kansas-Nebraska Act with its popular sovereignty provision, they were satisfied with merely the *possibility* of slavery in all the territories (how many, if any, would depend on the vote of the people living in them); this was in 1854.

But in 1857, the Supreme Court of the United States handed down a decision in the *Dred Scott* case, holding that Congress, under the Constitution, could not prohibit slavery in *any* of the territories, thereby opening them all to slavery, and putting an end to popular sovereignty.

But Chief Justice Roger B. Taney did more than that in his *Dred Scott* opinion—he opened a far fairer prospect for the Southern Democrats: slavery everywhere, not only in all the territories, but in all the *states*, north as well as south, new as well as old, Illinois as well as Kentucky, Massachusetts as well as Mississippi. How real a prospect was this? All it needed was another Supreme Court decision, and *Dred Scott* paved the way for that. As Lincoln put it, if *Dred Scott*, why not its sequel? Or, if the Chief Justice could dare the one, why could he not dare the other?

What Taney said in *Dred Scott* about the nationalization of slavery was only dicta, not part of the holding in the case, but it was not nothing there. He must have had some reason for making the statement; there is no reason to believe it was inadvertent; it is too deliberate for that. This is what he said: "The right of property in a slave is distinctly and expressly affirmed in the Constitution."

Taney was the Chief Justice of the United States, and, there-fore, his word carried some weight. Still, his saying it didn't make it so, not yet, and it certainly was not then so. The Constitution certainly did not say, or even imply, what Taney said it said. The late professor Herbert Storing put this very well: "If one had to think of two adverbs that do *not* describe the way the Constitution acknowledged slavery, he could not do better than 'distinctly and expressly.'"

Whatever else it was, Taney's statement proved to be grist for Lincoln's mill. He seized on it during the debates with Douglas in 1858, and rang the changes on it. He began with the Supremacy Clause of the Constitution (art. VI, clause 2), which provides (in part) that the Constitution is the supreme law of the land, and that "the judges of every state shall be bound thereby anything in the constitution or laws of any state to the contrary notwithstanding." He then constructed the following syllogism:

> Nothing in the constitution or laws of any state can destroy a right distinctly and expressly affirmed in the Constitution of the United States.

> The right of property in a slave is distinctly and expressly affirmed in the Constitution of the United States.

> Therefore, nothing in the constitution or laws of any state can destroy the right of property in a slave.

Q.E.D., *quod erat demonstrandum*. And what had Lincoln demonstrated? Assuming Taney spoke for them, the Southerners wanted slavery nationalized, i.e., protected by the Constitution in all the states of the United States. And beyond that, assuming Senators Crittenden and Jefferson Davis also spoke for them, they wanted slavery to be extended throughout the length and breadth of the Americas; the only limits being the slaveholders' appetite (or, they would say, their need) and the military power of the United States.

This, I suggest, is why Lincoln said *no* to the Crittenden compromise, or so-called compromise. And who—or who now—can blame him?

As to that, I wonder if we—we today—are not inclined to ignore or discount the very real possibility of slavery becoming lawful in all the states. Suppose the Republican party had heeded the advice of Horace Greeley and other Eastern Republicans and had supported Senator Douglas in his reelection campaign in 1858. Douglas had won their favor by his opposition to the fraudulent pro-slavery constitution proposed for Kansas, the so-called Lecompton Constitution. Had the Republicans supported Douglas, there would have been no Lincoln-Douglas debates, and, therefore, no "Freeport question" from Lincoln: "May the people of a Territory, in any lawful way, against the wish of a citizen of the United States, exclude slavery from its limits prior to the formation of a State constitution?" That was the question Lincoln asked at Freeport, and by answering it, by saying that—despite the *Dred Scott* decision—the people might exclude slavery from the territory, Douglas lost the support of the Southern Democrats, which, in turn, caused the split in the party in 1860 and led to the election of Lincoln.

Imagine an administration in Washington led by a man (Douglas) who did not care whether slavery was voted up or down, and supported by a party most of whose members wanted very much that it be voted up. What would have been the consequences?

And, once again employing the faint-hearted Horace Greeley as a foil, suppose Lincoln had heeded Greeley's advice and entered into peace negotiations with the Confederates in the spring or summer of 1864, *without* insisting, as Lincoln always did, on the abolition of slavery. The Confederates would surely have jumped at the chance, as well as the Northern people, who had grown more and more weary of the war—they had taken to singing "When This Cruel War Is Over" (a million copies of it had been sold)—and were obviously yearning for peace. They surely had reason to think it a cruel war. In six weeks, beginning May 3, at the Wilderness, and continuing at Spotsylvania (May 10–14), and Cold Harbor (June 1),Grant's Army of the Potomac had lost some 65,000 men killed, wounded, or missing in action—7,000 in a single afternoon, at Cold Harbor.

"Our bleeding, bankrupt, almost dying country," Greeley wrote Lincoln, "yearns for peace—shudders at the prospect of fresh conscriptions, of further wholesale devastations, and of new rivers of human blood. . . . I entreat you to submit overtures for peace to the Southern insurgents." But Lincoln refused to do so. By making abolition a condition for peace, Greeley said, Lincoln gave "new strength to the Democrats." So he did. As one Democrat wrote, "Tens of thousands of white men must yet bite the dust to allay the Negro mania of the President." And the Democratic party, meeting in Chicago in August 1864, adopted a peace platform in which they pledged to "preserve the rights of the States unimpaired" (meaning the states' right to hold slaves). The situation was such that Lincoln expected to be beaten, "and unless some great change takes place," he said, "*badly* beaten." Even the abolitionists were against him. Wendell Phillips declared that he would "cut off both hands before doing anything to aid Lincoln's reelection."

Who, then—besides Lincoln—was for continuing the war, at so terrible a price? Surely not the troops, who were deserting in droves, and not many of the officers. As one general said—this was after Cold Harbor—"For thirty days it has been one funeral process past me, and it has been too much." Yet Lincoln, though almost alone, was intransigent, just as he had been in 1861.

But suppose he had agreed to sue for peace, a peace without conditions, a peace whereby the Union would have been as it was before the war, but with slavery more safely secured than ever in those states that wanted it, and its champions agitating for its extension. What would have been the consequences of that?

———∞———

I earlier attributed our extraordinary interest in Lincoln, and especially our esteem for him, partly to what he said and how he said it. He was surely a great writer and speaker of words; in my judgment, the greatest. As I have said on another occasions, he was (and is) our national poet. In saying this, I referred initially—because of their emotional appeal—to some of his private letters, the one to Mrs. Bixby, for instance, or my favorite, the letter of condolence to the teenaged Fanny McCullough, whose father, Lincoln's friend from Illiinois, had been killed in battle. But I know no better way to demonstrate his poetic gifts, or the awesome beauty of his words, than by quoting the closing paragraph of his First Inaugural Address, March 4, 1861.

The Address was written, we know, in Springfield, before he departed for Washington. We have also been told, and have reason to believe, that every speech that carries his name was, in fact, written by him; he employed no speech writer. And we know from his law partner William Herndon that Lincoln was "inflexibly" opposed to changes in what he had written, especially on this occasion, because he was anxious to avoid any words that might "fan the flames of secession."

The closing paragraph in the Address might be an exception, an exception that can be said to prove the rule. The idea for it, or its central metaphor, was written and given to Lincoln by Senator Seward (soon to be Secretary of State). This is what Seward suggested that he say:

> I close. We are not, we must not be aliens or enemies but fellow countrymen and brethren. Although passion has strained our bonds of affection too hardly they must not, I am sure they will not be broken. The mystic chords of memory which proceeding from so many battlefields and so many patriot graves pass through all the hearts and all the hearths in this broad continent of ours will yet again harmonize in their ancient music when breathed upon by the guardian angels of the nation.

And this is what Lincoln said:

> I am loth to close. We are not enemies, but friends. We must not be enemies. Though passion may have

strained, it must not break our bonds of affection. The mystic chords of memory, stretching from every battle-field, and patriot grave, to every living heart and hearth-stone, all over this broad land, will yet swell the chorus of the Union, when again touched, as surely they will be, by the better angels of our nature.

It is not by chance that his best and most celebrated speech was delivered on a battlefield, on the occasion of dedicating a cemetery filled with the graves of patriots. I speak, of course, of the Gettysburg Address.

A prefatory statement before turning to the Address: The principles of the Constitution are set down in the Declaration of Independence, a document that appeals to the "laws of Nature and of Nature's God," a god—arguably, at least—that reveals himself not in the Bible but in the "book of nature," the book readable in our day by astrophysicists and in those days by the Enlightenment philosophers and their students, such as Thomas Jefferson. What Lincoln did at Gettysburg was to make something else of the Declaration: a statement of fundamental principles—"our ancient faith," as he put it—to which we were attached not only with our minds, but also with our hearts.

The Gettysburg Address is brief, a mere 272 words, and could not have taken much more than five minutes to deliver. In its central passage, Lincoln says, "The world will little note, nor long remember what we say here, but it can never forget what they did here." Well, what little do we remember?

We remember he said that this nation was founded in 1776 with the Declaration of Independence and its principles. We remember this because of the unusual way he said it. Not eighty-seven years ago, but "fourscore and seven." His Bible-reading audience assembled there (and afterwards) would surely have remembered what he said because they would have heard echoes of the ninetieth Psalm, where the Psalmist says that our years on this earth are "three score and ten," and "four score" if we're healthy. They would not have known that the principles we declared in

1776 had their wellspring not in the Bible, but in the second of John Locke's *Two Treatises of Government*, and that Locke's connection with us is confirmed by the fact that his words are—although without attribution—three times quoted in our Declaration; they would not have been told this because our association-one-with-another is supposed to be something more exalted than a Lockean contract entered into by anti-social individuals seeking only to secure their private rights. (Did Lincoln not speak of us as friends?) They might have thought instead—because of the implied association with the Bible, as well as Lincoln's designation of the Founders as "our Fathers" (who art in heaven?), as they probably were expected to think—that our founding, if not sacred, was surely not profane.

They (Lincoln's Bible-reading audience) might also have believed this because—and this, too, we remember—Lincoln goes on to say, after suggesting that the nation so founded might not long endure, that the brave men, living and dead, who struggled on this ground, this battlefield, had "consecrated" it better than he or anyone else could. Consecrated? Had made it sacred, a battlefield? As if they—presumably the Union soldiers—were fighting for the Lord? No, but their cause was great and noble.

We also remember Lincoln saying that their work was "unfinished," and that we, the living, should highly resolve that these dead shall not have died in vain and that this nation, "under God, shall have a new birth of freedom," and that government of, by, and for the people shall not perish from the earth.

What little do we remember? In a word, and despite what he said, we remember everything he said, and we remember it because he took great pains to say it beautifully, to the end that we remember it.

We also remember his Second Inaugural address, especially the concluding paragraph—the poignant beauty of it:

> With malice toward none; with charity for all; with firmness in the right, as God gives us to see right, let us strive on to finish the work we are in; to bind up the nation's

wounds; to care for him who shall have borne the battle, and for his widow, and his orphan—to do all which may achieve and cherish a just, and a lasting peace, among ourselves, and with all nations.

Six weeks later, he was murdered.

———

We say that a man can be known by the company he keeps. So I say that a nation, a people, can be known and be judged by its heroes, by whom it honors above all others.

We pay ourselves the greatest compliment when we say that Abraham Lincoln is that man for us.

Walter Berns
February 9, 2009

About the Author

Walter Berns is a professor emeritus at Georgetown University and a resident scholar at the American Enterprise Institute. He has taught at the University of Toronto, the University of Chicago (where he earned a PhD in political science), and Cornell and Yale universities. His government service includes membership on the National Council on the Humanities, the Council of Scholars in the Library of Congress, and the Judicial Fellows Commission, and in 1983 he was the alternate United States representative to the United Nations Commission on Human Rights. He has been a Guggenheim, Rockefeller, and Fulbright Fellow and a Phi Beta Kappa lecturer. He is the author of numerous articles on American government and politics in both professional and popular journals; his many books include *In Defense of Liberal Democracy*, *The First Amendment and the Future of American Democracy*, *Taking the Constitution Seriously*, *Making Patriots*, and *Democracy and the Constitution*. President George W. Bush awarded him the 2005 National Humanities Medal for his scholarship on the history of the Constitution.

Printed in the USA
CPSIA information can be obtained
at www.ICGtesting.com
LVHW011540240824
789107LV00007B/203